DISCOVERING

BRAZIL

By Marion Morrison

A ZOË BOOK

A ZOË BOOK

Devised and produced by
Zoë Books Limited
15 Worthy Lane
Winchester
Hampshire SO23 7AB
England

First published in Great Britain in 1996 by
Zoë Books Limited
15 Worthy Lane
Winchester
Hampshire SO23 7AB

A record of the CIP data is available from the British Library.

ISBN 1 874488 62 2

Printed in Italy by Grafedit SpA
Editor: Kath Davies
Design: Jan Sterling, Sterling Associates
Map: Gecko Limited
Production: Grahame Griffiths

Photographic acknowledgments
The publishers wish to acknowledge, with thanks, the following photographic sources:

South American Pictures / Tony Morrison - Cover, title page, 5, 7, 8, 9, 10, 11, 12, 13, 14, 15, 16, 17, 18, 19, 20, 21r, 22, 23l, 24, 27l, 28, 29; / Marion Morrison - 25l; Bill Leimbach - 6; 23r, 25r, 26, 27r; Hutchison Library/Michael MacIntyre 21l.

The publishers have made every attempt to trace the copyright holders, but if they have inadvertently overlooked any, they will be pleased to make the necessary arrangement at the first opportunity.

Cover: *Carnival in Río de Janeiro*

Title page: *Sunset on Maria Farinha Island, near Recife*

Contents

Brazil

Area: 8 547 404 sq km
(3 300 171 sq miles)
Population: 159 000 000 (1994)
Capital: Brasília

Bem vindo!

Welcome to Brazil! Brazil is the world's fifth largest country, and has the world's sixth largest population. This country covers almost half of the South American continent and shares borders with ten countries. French Guiana, Surinam, Guyana and Venezuela lie to the north of Brazil. Colômbia is in the north west, while Peru and Bolivia are west and southwest of the country. Paraguay, Argentina and Uruguay lie to the south. Only Ecuador and Chile do not share a frontier with Brazil.

Brazil's east coast faces the Atlantic Ocean and is more than 7000 km (4375 miles) long. Most of Brazil lies between the Equator and the Tropic of Capricorn. From its east Atlantic coast Brazil extends across the continent to within 550 km (345 miles) of the Pacific Ocean. It is a vast land of rivers, highlands, plains, and tropical rainforests.

The old town of Pariti on the Atlantic coast

Brazilians in national colours celebrate at the Río carnival after winning the World Cup

The 'greatest show on Earth'

There are many things for which Brazil is famous. Perhaps at the top of the list is football, especially after Brazil won the World Cup for a record fourth time in 1994. However, many people when they think of Brazil, think of the Amazon, which is the world's greatest river. Around the Amazon lie the rainforests that house one-quarter of all known plant species.

The carnival which is held every year in Río de Janeiro has been called the 'greatest show on Earth'.

Brazil's modern capital, Brasília, was founded in 1960. It was built in a remote area of the country, and is also one of the wonders of Brazil.

The Amazon Basin

The Amazon Basin is almost as large as the United States of America. Most of the Basin is in Brazil, but long tributaries also flow from neighbouring countries to join the main Amazon river. Seventeen tributaries are each more than 1500 km (940 miles) long. The longest is the Madeira from Bolivia, which runs for more than 3300 km (2065 miles).

Every second, the River Amazon pours 10 billion litres (2.2 billion gallons) of water into the Atlantic Ocean. The force of the water at the river's mouth is so strong that it pushes the salt water back into the ocean for 150 kilometres (95 miles). When explorers first discovered this fresh water in the sea, they called it the 'Sweet Water Sea'. The mouth of the Amazon is more than 320 km (200 miles) wide. It is so large that within it lies an island, Marajó, the size of Switzerland.

The towns

Much of the Amazon Basin is covered with tropical rainforest, but there are also grasslands, scrub forests and swamps. The largest city and port is Manaus, 1500 km (940 miles) upstream, where about one million people live. Manaus is at the 'meeting of the waters', where the tea-coloured water of the Río Negro meets the white water of the Amazon.

Belém, on the mouth of the river, is another important city and port. Pôrto Velho in the western state of Rondônia is growing fast. It is at the centre of a region where the forest is being cut down for timber and cattle-grazing. Many settlers are moving here from other parts of Brazil.

Kayapo Indians of the Xingu, shooting fish from a canoe on the Amazon

The rainforest

The rainforest is a dense mass of plants and trees. Many of the trees are over 45 metres (148 feet) high, with smooth straight trunks. Their branches begin far from the ground and bear a thick layer of leaves that catch the sunlight.

This evergreen canopy also contains other plants such as mosses, and massive lianas that send out long roots to reach the ground. There are also plants called *bromeliads*, which belong to the same plant family as the pineapple.

Some of the tallest trees include the brazilnut and the silk cotton trees, whose tops stretch above the canopy. There are also hardwood trees, such as mahogany. The temperature in the rainforest is usually about 27°C, and most days each year the forest is soaked with rain.

Lianas in the Amazon rainforest

A toucan in the rainforest

The wildlife

The River Amazon has more than 3000 species of fish. The forest is home to thousands of species of insect, including brilliant butterflies such as the Morphos. The largest mammal is the tapir, and there are deer both large and small. Monkeys live high in the canopy. Most of them have a tail that can be used like a hand to grasp the branches. Also in the canopy are many birds. The flowers attract hummingbirds, while toucans feed on fruits and parrots find nuts and berries.

At one time, the rivers were home to large South American alligators, called caimans, but many have disappeared through trapping. Of the snakes, the largest is the anaconda which can be seven metres (23 feet) long. The smallest snakes are no thicker than bootlaces and hide among the hanging vines.

The coast and the highlands

A view of the coast between Río de Janeiro and São Paulo

Brazil has the longest coastline in the world, with many fine, white-sand beaches. There are beautiful islands offshore, such as the rocky group, or archipelago, of Fernando de Noronha. Near the Amazon mouth there are forests. Further north, mangroves extend along a muddy shoreline for hundreds of kilometres. In the far south are coastal lagoons.

Between the cities of Salvador and Pôrto Alegre rise the steep slopes of the Great Escarpment. Brazil's two largest cities, São Paulo and Río de Janeiro, are within this small, fertile area. They contain more than one-third of the total population of Brazil.

Highlands

In the far north of Brazil are the Guiana Highlands. They are part of a larger mountain area, which extends into the nearby countries of the Guianas and Venezuela. It is here that Brazil's highest mountain, the mist-shrouded Pico da Neblina rises 3014 metres (9889 feet) from the northern rim of the Amazon Basin. Other highlands extend from the southern edge of the Amazon Basin across the central part of the country, southwards towards Uruguay. The central region includes the forest and scrubland area known as the Mato Grosso, and the highland plain on which the capital Brasília is located. The highest point in southern Brazil is the Pico da Bandeira, at 2890 metres (9482 feet) above sea level.

Herding cattle in northeast Brazil

The northeast

The northeast of Brazil receives very little rainfall and suffers from long periods of drought. Known to Brazilians as the backlands, or *sertão*, the region is covered with a forest of thorny bushes, low trees and cactus plants. This vegetation is known as the *caatinga* and is very inhospitable. In some places, over thousands of years, the rocks have been worn down, or eroded, by wind, sun and rain. Early explorers mistook these curious shapes for castles. Between the driest land near the coast and the Amazon Basin to the west is a region where there is more vegetation. A large river, the Parnaíba, flows through it to the Atlantic Ocean.

River São Francisco

The São Francisco river is 2900 km (1815 miles) long and flows through the eastern part of Brazil. It is the longest river that begins and ends in Brazil and is considered to be the National River of the country.

Two great rivers

The River Paraguay begins in a huge swamp in the far west of Brazil. The land here is a low-lying region of lakes and rivers known as the *pantanal*. It is famous for its thousands of birds, caimans and other wildlife. The Paraguay flows south into the Paraná, a 3900 km (2440 miles) long river with its source in the highlands of southern Brazil. Close to where the borders of Brazil, Argentina and Paraguay meet, on a small tributary of the Paraná, are the 275 waterfalls, or cataracts, that make up the magnificent Iguazú Falls.

The Iguazú Falls

On the ranch

Brazil has a large beef and dairy industry. The main cattle-raising regions are in the south, where open grasslands extend to neighbouring Uruguay and Argentina.

The state of Rio Grande do Sul is the land of the cowboys, or *gauchos*. They herd millions of cattle, sheep and pigs on large ranches, or *estancias*, of thousands of hectares. Their traditional dress includes baggy trousers, called *bombachas*, knee-high leather boots and a long leather apron to protect their legs. A *gaucho* never goes to work without his *maté*, which is a bitter herbal tea made by pouring hot water (carried in a thermos) on to *maté* leaves, and sipped through a metal straw.

Cattle are also raised in northeast Brazil. In this arid, poor region, the cowboys, or *vaqueiros*, wear leather hats and trousers to protect themselves against the spiny cacti and the thorny scrub vegetation on which the cattle graze. Wide areas of rainforest have also been cleared for cattle raising, but the pasture is often not good enough to feed large numbers of animals.

Cultivating crops

Only 20 per cent of Brazil's land is used for farming. Yet Brazil is the world's leading producer and exporter of both coffee and sugar. Coffee grows on the hilly slopes west of Río de Janeiro and São Paulo, in the south. A small amount grows in the Amazon region. Sometimes, an entire year's coffee crop is spoiled by severe frosts. This pushes up the price of

Cowboys on a ranch in southern Brazil

coffee throughout the world. Brazil grows many varieties of fruit, and supplies 85 per cent of the world's concentrated orange juice. Other crops include tobacco, cocoa, cotton, maize and nuts. Brazil grows most of the food it needs, but it still has to import wheat.

Fruits of Brazil

açaí – is a palm tree that provides 'heart of palm', or *palmito*, and fruit that is used for juices, ice-cream and wine;

brazilnuts – were first taken to Europe in 1633;

cupuaçu – is used for soft drinks, juices, ice-cream, sweets, wine and liqueurs;

guava – was first grown in the Americas and is now widespread throughout the world;

maracujá – or passionfruit – is used in soft drinks and ice-cream.

Picking ripe coffee berries

Mahogany planks in a timber yard, Belém

Felling the forest

In recent years, large areas of the Amazon forest have been cut down. Hardwoods such as mahogany are highly valued in the furniture trade and are exported to the USA and to Europe. Softwoods, such as parana pine and eucalyptus, are grown in the southern regions. They supply the local pulp and paper industry. Most of the country's woods are used as fuel.

Fishing

Fish is an important source of food, but Brazil's fishing industry is small. The largest catches are of cod, lobster, crab and shrimp.

Industry and energy

Brazil is rich in minerals including iron ore, lead, gold and platinum. The Carajás iron-ore deposit was discovered in the Amazon in 1967. It is believed to hold the world's largest iron-ore reserves. Carajás also has bauxite, manganese and copper. Ninety per cent of the world market's semi-precious gems, such as amethyst and topaz, come from Brazil.

Fifty years ago, Brazil relied on coffee as its main source of income. Industrial production now accounts for 60 per cent of all Brazil's exports. Most of the factories are in the southeast, around São Paulo. People make all kinds of goods, including ships, cars and aircraft, refrigerators and washing machines. Textiles and processed food and drink are also important. Many new industries make electronic and computer goods, for which there is a big demand.

The energy which Brazil needs to run its industries comes from hydro-electricity, coal, gas and oil. Ninety-two per cent of the country's electricity comes from water power. The largest hydro-electric plant, Itaipú, is on the Paraná river. The walls of the Itaipú dam are 165 metres (540 feet) thick and the dam is 190 metres (623 feet) high. With the completion of the second stage of the dam in 1990, its output of 12.600MW was the greatest of any dam in the world.

Brazil is also the third largest producer of crude oil in Latin America. Most of its reserves lie in offshore fields.

The iron-ore mine at Carajás

A new hotel at Recife

Tourism

Río de Janeiro is known for its beautiful beaches, the nearby Sugar Loaf mountain and the huge statue of Christ that overlooks the city. For many years, Río has been a favourite city for tourists. Every year, the Carnival in Río attracts many thousands of visitors.

Less well known are the hundreds of kilometres of wonderful beaches, small bays and tiny forested islands that line the coast of Brazil. Much of the coast is still undeveloped, but in the northeast around Recife and Fortaleza luxury hotels and apartments are being built for tourists. Other popular places are the Amazon and the spectacular Iguazú Falls. About one million tourists visit Brazil every year. Most visitors come from other parts of Latin America, and from the USA and Canada.

Getting around

The main problem in getting around Brazil is the size of the country. Even by air it can still take six to seven hours to fly from Florianópolis in the south to Belém on the Amazon. Brazil has several national airlines. They have many flights a day within Brazil, and international flights to all parts of the world. Small airlines also make regular trips to remote areas.

The most dramatic change in transport has come about with the building of good highways, particularly across the Amazon region. Road transport now carries 60 per cent of the country's freight and 95 per cent of passengers. Brazil also has an excellent long-distance bus service. There are few railways. In some remote regions, people still have to rely on river transport as their only means of getting around.

Many cars in Brazil use 'alcool' instead of petrol. This fuel is made from sugarcane.

People and language

A crowd of Brazilians watching the carnival in Río de Janeiro

The population of Brazil is about 159 million people and it is very mixed. A very few people are American Indians. Their ancestors were the first people to live in the country. Most Brazilians are descendants of various groups of people who have settled there during the last 500 years. The Portuguese explorers arrived in the sixteenth century, when Brazil became a Portuguese colony.

At that time the American Indians probably numbered between one and two million. Today there are thought to be less than 150 000 native people. During the 1600s and 1700s, sugar plantations provided most of the country's wealth. Slaves were brought from Africa to work on these plantations. The population grew slowly. By the middle of the 1800s, only four million people lived in Brazil.

The African tradition is still strong in Brazil. In Salvador, black women, dressed in the traditional white costume of their ancestors, sell African-style food on the city streets. There are several African-Brazilian forms of religion, and the African beat is strong in Brazilian music and dance.

Immigrants

From about 1850, immigrants began to arrive in Brazil. They were mainly Italian, Portuguese, Spanish and German. Later, Slavs arrived from Poland, Russia and the Ukraine, and Arabs from the Middle East. Many of the Europeans settled in the south and became farmers. Today, there are many communities in this

Blumenau, a German community in southern Brazil

region whose culture is still largely European. The most significant immigrant group to arrive since 1900 have been the Japanese. They are very successful in business, particularly in the coffee, cotton and tea trades.

Indians

Many thousands of American Indians died from diseases which the Europeans brought to Brazil. Today, scattered tribes still live in the Amazon and in the north. Their way of life is still largely traditional, though some people now use guns instead of bows and arrows. They use metal pots and tools, they own radios and a few have television. They hunt and

Squeezing the poison out of manioc, before it is cooked

fish, and cultivate gardens, where they grow potatoes, maize, beans and *manioc*. *Manioc* is their main, or staple, food which is made into bread.

The American Indians are still being threatened, even in their own lands. Some people are trying to gain control of their land, to sell it or to make money out of it by felling the timber. New roads also bring changes to the people's way of life. Some American Indians have died fighting for their land.

Language

Portuguese is the official language of Brazil, but it has taken in both African and American Indian words. There are four main American Indian languages, and many local dialects.

Living in Brazil

The east side of Brazil was the first to be settled. It has always been the most densely populated. The southeast has the big cities and the best farmland. The northeast is very dry, there are few jobs and the people are poor. Three-quarters of the population now live in towns and cities, and half of these people live in Río de Janeiro and São Paulo. In the cities, people work in factories, as teachers, doctors and lawyers, in government jobs, or they may be taxi drivers or maids.

Outside the cities, people have to work hard on the land to survive. As a result, in recent years thousands of people have moved from the country into the cities. Many people have been disappointed in their search for a better life. There are too few houses, schools or hospitals to cope with such large numbers of people. Most of them have to live in cardboard and corrugated iron shacks on the outskirts of the towns. Often, these shanty towns, called *favelas*, have no electricity, water or proper sanitation.

Family life

Families in Brazil are very close. Among the poorer people it is often the only way to survive. Frequently three generations live in one house. The grandparents often look after the young children. Many young children have to find jobs to help the family income. In the cities they work at cleaning cars, or running errands, while in rural areas they work on the land.

Favelas and skyscrapers, Río de Janeiro

Padre Cicero

Padre Cicero was a popular priest from the northeast of Brazil. He worked among the poor. In 1890 he was thought to have worked a miracle. The church authorities disagreed, and banned him from the church. The people, however, believed that he did have special powers. Every year thousands of pilgrims visit the town of Juàzeiro do Norte. They come to see the huge statue of Padre Cicero, and to pray to him.

Religion

Officially, 90 per cent of the Brazilian people are Christians who belong to the Roman Catholic church. However, many Brazilians practise a religion that combines Catholicism, African and American Indian beliefs. Religions of African origin, such as *candomblé*, *macumba* and *umbanda*, have a large following, especially in Salvador and Río de Janeiro.

Food

What you eat in Brazil depends on where you are. The far south is cattle country where, as the *gauchos* say, they eat meat for breakfast, lunch and dinner. In the Amazon, fish is the main source of food and the razor-toothed pirana makes a tasty dish. The state of Bahía has African food. There, recipes include seafood such as lobster and shrimp, palm oil, coconut milk, nuts and peppers.

Selling African food in Salvador

Main cities

A fruit stall in front of banks and offices, São Paulo

São Paulo is Brazil's fastest growing city. Its population of 19 million is larger than any other city in South America. It was founded in 1554 by two priests as a mission station. About 100 years ago, São Paulo was still a small town of mud-brick buildings, with a population of 30 000. In the later 1800s, wealthy landowners began to put money into businesses in the city.

At the beginning of the twentieth century, many thousands of immigrants settled in the region. Their hard work created much agricultural wealth, and the city became an important business centre. São Paulo is now Brazil's main industrial centre. The city has a very good supply of hydro-electric power. São Paulo produces 40 per cent of the country's industrial production, but it consumes 60 per cent of the country's electricity.

Concrete and glass skyscrapers rise in the centre of São Paulo. There are few old historic buildings. The city streets are always busy with shoppers and business people. In the outer areas, or suburbs, are some of the largest shopping centres in South America. São Paulo has many tree-filled squares and parks. However, the city's industrial factories and thousands of cars are polluting the air.

Brasília

Brasília became the new capital of Brazil on 21 April 1960. It was built in a remote area, with the aim of opening up

The Palace of Congress, Brasília

the centre of the country. More than a million people now live in Brasília. All the country's political buildings are in Brasília. They include the twin-towered Congress building, the government Ministries, the President's Palace and the splendid Ministry of Foreign Affairs with its sculptures and water gardens.

People live in specially designed housing, and there are schools and shops nearby. There are also well laid out areas for business, for hotels and for entertainment. But Brasília is not an easy city to walk around, because of the wide open spaces, long avenues and very hot climate.

Santos

Brazil's most important port is 63 km (39 miles) from São Paulo. Santos handles more than 40 per cent of Brazil's imports, and about half of its exports.

Río de Janeiro

The Brazilians say, 'God made the world in six days, the seventh he devoted to Río'. Stretched out along the coast, the city is built up behind white sand beaches. The green slopes of the forested eastern highlands rise behind Río.

Río has well designed gardens and parks, and old and interesting suburbs like Santa Teresa. New skyscrapers tower over small colonial buildings. The roads are full of noisy traffic. Shanty houses perch on the hillsides above the city. There is the magnificent Sugar Loaf mountain, and many beaches, such as Copacabana, Ipanema and Leblon, which are always full of sunbathers. But Río also has a dark side. Crime, poverty and pollution are growing problems. The city is struggling to cope with its rapidly increasing population.

Sugar Loaf mountain and Botafogo Bay, Río

Arts and leisure

Brazil's best known twentieth-century artist is Cândido Portinari. He was born in 1903 of a poor immigrant family. Many of his paintings depict scenes from Brazil, such as the coffee plantations or poor peasants in the north-east.

Many people consider Brazil's spectacular modern architecture to be its most striking artistic achievement. The exciting modern buildings of Brasília have attracted worldwide attention. For example, the Cathedral is shaped like a 'crown of thorns', and much of the interior is below street level. Most buildings were designed and built by Lúcio Costa and Oscar Neimeyer. Many stand in well laid out gardens and lawns, the work of landscape designer Roberto Burle Marx.

Sculptors

In Brasília there are many works by modern sculptors, such as Alfredo Ceschiatti and Bruno Giorgi. Giorgi's enormous sculpture, *The Warriors*, stands in front of the President's office. Perhaps, though, the most remarkable of Brazil's sculptors was Antônio Francisco Lisbôa, otherwise known as Aleijadinho, or 'the little cripple'. He lived in the eighteenth century and was the child of a Portuguese carpenter and a black slave woman. His greatest works include a tableau of the Last Supper and twelve lifesize statues of the prophets which can still be seen today outside a church near the town of Ouro Prêto.

'The Last Supper' by Aleijadinho

A football match in Río

'Futebol'

Brazilian people love football. From a very early age, young children kick a ball around. It does not matter where, maybe on the beach, in the streets or on any spare patch of ground. For the lucky few, to be a professional footballer is a sure way of making a fortune. Río has the largest football stadium in the world, the Maracana, which holds 155 000 people. There are more than 20 000 soccer teams in Brazil, with regular matches in every village, town and city. Important matches are followed closely by almost everybody, and a win means that there will be many parties. For a match like the World Cup final, the whole nation simply stops work to watch!

Pelé

Probably the greatest footballer of all time, Pelé was in the first three Brazilian teams to win the World Cup. In a 21-year career, from the time he was 15, he scored a total of 1200 goals in national and international matches.

Other stars

Brazil's tennis star, Maria Bueno, was Wimbledon champion three times, and won the US Open Championship four times in the 1960s.

In Grand Prix racing, Emerson Fittipaldi was World Champion twice in the 1970s. Nelson Piquet was Champion three times in the 1980s. When Ayrton Senna died in 1994, only 34 years old, he had already been World Champion three times.

Keeping fit, Copacabana Beach

Carnival!

Carnival takes place all over Brazil, either in late February or in early March. The most spectacular parade is in Río de Janeiro. About 80 000 people take part, singing and dancing in the streets to the music of the samba. The dancers belong to samba schools from different parts of the city. A large samba school may have 5000 dancers and 400 musicians. The schools compete to be the Carnival champions. The Carnival parade takes place over two nights in Río's specially built Sambadrome. Each school does its best to impress the judges. All the fans of the samba schools cheer, sing and dance as their teams perform. Río remains anxious until the result is announced a few days later.

Religious festivals

Brazilians enjoy many of the Christian festivals such as Christmas, Easter, and many saints' days. The African religions also hold festivals. Probably the best known is the festival of Iemanjá, the African goddess of the sea. In Río de Janeiro, at midnight on New Year's Eve, followers of the religion *umbanda*, mostly dressed in white, wade into the sea with flowers and gifts on tiny boats as offerings. They hope the gifts will be washed out to sea, as this is a sign that the goddess has accepted them.

The Beija Flor Samba School in the carnival parade, Río

Capoeira *dancing, Ipanema beach, Río*

Music and dance

The music and dance of Brazil come from many different places. The Portuguese brought instruments such as the accordion, viola, guitar and tambourine. Many folk songs and dances also date back to early colonial history. Traditional African instruments include the *berimbau*, which is shaped like an archer's bow, and is played by striking a stick across the wire or 'bowstring'. It is used to accompany *capoeira*, a sort of kicking and leaping martial arts dance. American Indians have rattles made from gourds and pipes. Some pipes are more than a metre (3 feet) long, and one used only on special occasions, is over three metres (9 feet) long. Heitor Villa-Lobos, Brazil's most famous composer, used folk songs, Indian-style instruments and the beat of African drums in his music.

TV and film

In the 1940s, the film *That Night In Rio*, brought worldwide fame for the actress Carmen Miranda. In her sequined dress, platform shoes and exotic headdress, she was the soul of Brazilian music and dance.

Films and televison are very popular in Brazil today. Not everyone can afford to own a television, but they share with neighbours and friends. The television is sometimes used to send educational programmes to people in remote areas. The most popular programmes are 'soap operas' or *novelas*. These are often shown three times a day to audiences of about 80 million people.

Street musicians in Recife

From colony to independence

The altar inside the Church of São Francisco, Salvador

On 22 April 1500, the Portuguese Admiral, Pedro Alvarez Cabral, landed on the coast of Brazil. He had left Portugal to sail to India, and it is not known why he strayed so far off course that he reached South America. Cabral was met by friendly American Indians, and one of his first acts was to hold a Christian service. He christened the newly discovered territory 'Land of the True Cross', but it soon became 'Brazil'. It was named after the brazilwood tree which was sent to Europe. A red dye was made from the wood of this tree.

Colonial Brazil

The Portuguese colonists settled in the east of Brazil, where they founded the town of Salvador. Sugarcane grew well, and the colonists tried to force the American Indians to work on plantations. When the Indians resisted, large numbers were killed. Instead, black slaves were brought from Africa. Within a few years, Brazil was the world's main sugar producer.

During the 1700s, armed bands of pioneers called *bandeirantes* explored the wilderness west of São Paulo for gold and diamonds. They opened up trails and set up trading posts. This was the first

Brazilian 'gold rush', and it brought large numbers of prospectors from Europe. Soon Brazil was supplying half the world's gold. Many colonists moved into southern Brazil, and in 1763, Río de Janeiro became the capital of the country.

A king in exile

By the second half of the 1700s, the colonists in Brazil did not want to be ruled from Portugal. In 1789 the first revolt against the Portuguese was led by a young soldier who was called Tiradentes, the 'toothpuller'. The revolt failed and Tiradentes was executed. However, in 1807 the Portuguese Prince Regent (later King João VI) was forced into exile in Brazil. The prince fell in love with his new country and he began to modernize it. He opened up trade with Europe and allowed all sorts of goods into Brazil for the first time. Tea, silver cutlery and fine cloth came from England. From France came wines, jewels and fashions. Dom João founded the first bank, newspaper, medical school, theatre, library and museum. He paved the streets and installed street lighting. He even introduced sea bathing! He refused to go back to Portugal until 1816, and then he left his son, Dom Pedro, behind as Prince Regent.

The statue of Tiradentes, Ouro Prêto

Independence

When the Portuguese government commanded the Prince Regent to return to Portugal, he too refused. He made a famous speech called the 'Cry', or *Grito*, of 'Independence or Death'. On 1 December 1822, he was proclaimed Emperor Dom Pedro I of Brazil.

Dom Pedro I

Empire and Republic

Dom Pedro I reigned only for nine years. He gave up the throne, or abdicated, in favour of his son who, in 1840, at the age of 15, was crowned Emperor Dom Pedro II. The young man was a wise ruler. Education and science were important to him. He was the first person in Brazil to have his photograph taken and the first to use the telephone. The first steam railway opened in 1859. Dom Pedro II encouraged other countries to put money into Brazil's businesses. He opened more banks to deal with the increase in business. He also invited immigrants from Europe to settle in Brazil.

Slavery

The slave trade with Africa ended in Brazil in 1850. The plantation owners, however, still depended on slaves as a workforce. Dom Pedro II wanted to abolish slavery, but he knew that the rich landowners would be against this. In 1888 he was away in Europe and his daughter Isabel was acting as Regent. She issued a decree to free all slaves in Brazil. But the slave owners conspired with the army and overthrew the Emperor. Dom Pedro and his family were sent into exile. In 1889, Brazil became a Republic. The Empire was over.

The monument to the Bandeirantes, São Paulo

The rubber boom

With the invention of the motor car, rubber was in great demand for tyres. The great Amazon rubber boom began! At the centre of the trade was the small town of Manaus. It became one of the grandest and most extravagant places on the continent, with hospitals, banks, a racecourse, the first telephone in the Amazon and a lavishly decorated Opera House. However, the fortunes spent in Manaus were made by forcing groups of American Indians into an endless grind of tapping rubber trees. The scandal was exposed. At the same time, rubber plantations were developing well in the Far East, from seeds secretly collected in the Amazon. The Amazon rubber boom collapsed in 1912.

The Opera House, Manaus

The Republic

Brazil became a republic on 15 November 1889. Instead of an emperor, there was a president, and the rules for governing Brazil were set out in the constitution. There were problems in the early years, and thirteen presidents held office between 1889 and 1930. During this period, a middle class began to emerge who wanted social reform. In 1930 they gave their support to Getúlio Vargas, in a military takeover that made him president. Vargas was known as 'The Father of the Poor' because he improved people's social and working conditions. But when he declared himself dictator in 1945, he was overthrown by the army.

The bandit, Lampiao (the 'lantern')

Brazil today

The campaign for first direct elections, 1985

In 1956 Juscelino Kubitschek became president of Brazil. His slogan was 'Fifty years progress in five'. Dams were built, the car industry was begun, and iron-ore exports were doubled. The building of the capital, Brasília, in a desolate area where there was no railway and only dirt roads was a huge task. The project left Brazil with a financial crisis. This led to another army takeover, and from 1964 to 1985 the military were in power.

The Brazilian miracle

The 'Brazilian miracle' occurred in the 1970s. In those years, large scale projects, including building the Itaipú Dam, finally made Brazil into a modern industrial nation. However, Brazil had to borrow money from other countries to build these projects. The 'miracle' left the country with enormous debts. Although there were thousands more jobs, the gap between rich and poor people continued to grow. Also, under military rule, people who disagreed with the generals were arrested and often tortured, killed, or sent into exile. Military rule ended in 1985, when it was clear that the people were not supporting the generals. In 1989 there were elections, and Fernando Collor became president. After two years in office, Collor was forced to resign on grounds of corruption, and was replaced by the Vice President, Itamar Franco. In the elections of 1994, the people chose Fernando Henrique Cardoso as their president.

The rainforest in the Amazon

Decades of destruction

Since the 1960s, large areas of the Amazon forest have been destroyed as governments have tried to develop the region. First the highways were built. Then people were offered money and land to persuade them to settle in the Amazon. Thousands of hectares of forest were cleared for cattle grazing. However, once the forest was cut down, the land was not as fertile as it had seemed. Farming and ranching were not very profitable.

The opening up of the Carajás iron mine led to road and railway building. The iron-ore smelters were fuelled by charcoal which meant further forest destruction. The gold prospectors polluted many rivers with mercury. The most recent threat to the forest is from some types of tree felling for the timber industry.

The future

In the 1990s the Brazilian government joined with other countries to try to protect its environment. In 1992, Brazil hosted the Rio 92 Earth Summit Conference, which was attended by more than 100 heads of state. The conference discussed threats to the environment and what could be done to preserve the world's plant and animal life. Brazil has already cut back on forest destruction and has set up more parks and nature reserves. Curitiba in the south has become a 'green' city, where children are being taught to care for their environment. Brazil still faces many problems but it has huge resources and great potential. The people of Brazil are looking forward to the 21st century.

Children at the Carnival in Río

Fact file

Government

Brazil is a federal republic consisting of 26 states and the Federal District of Brasília. Each state has an elected governor.

The government consists of two houses, the Senate, with 81 members, and the Chamber of Deputies, with 503 members. These two houses make up the National Congress.

Members of the Senate are elected for an eight year term, and members of the Chamber of Deputies for four years. Everyone over the age of 16 can vote.

The Brazilian head of state is the president. The president is elected every five years but cannot serve for two terms in succession.

Flag

Brazil's flag is green, yellow and blue. The central blue globe contains 23 stars which represent the original states of Brazil, and the words 'Order and Progress'.

National anthem

Brazil's national anthem is called *Hino do Ipiranga*.

Religion

About 90 per cent of Brazilians are officially Roman Catholic, but many also take part in African cult religions, such as *candomblé*, *macumba* and *umbanda*.

Money

The unit of Brazilian currency is the *Real*, or R$. One *Real* is made up of 100 *centavos*.

Education

Most schools in Brazil are run by the government or by the church, and are free. Other schools are paid for privately.

School is compulsory for all Brazilian children between the ages of seven and fourteen. Secondary education begins at 15 and lasts for four years, but very few pupils complete the courses.

There are over 90 universities in the country, but they are not well attended.

Newspapers

There are more than 250 daily newspapers in Brazil, but there is no national newspaper. Newspapers are published regionally. Most newspapers are sold in a large city such as *O Estado de São Paulo* in São Paulo, or *O Globo* in Río de Janeiro.

Broadcasting

The largest TV network in Brazil is TV Globo, which sometimes has audiences of over 80 million people. Favourite programmes are *novelas*, or 'soaps', but there are also many educational programmes. Satellite television and radio are now available in all parts of the country.

Some famous people

Tomé de Sousa (c.1515-73) was the first governor general of the Portuguese colony of Brazil
Aleijadinho (1738-1814) was an architect and sculptor
Pedro I (1798-1834) was the first emperor of Brazil
Pedro II (1825-91) ruled as emperor from 1840 to 1889
Antônio de Castro Alves (1847-71) was a poet
Cândido Mariano da Silva Rondon (1865-1958), an explorer who also founded the Indian Protection Service
Alberto Santos-Dumont (1873-1932) was a designer of early aircraft
Getúlio Vargas (1883-1954) was president from 1930-45, and 1950-54
Heitor Villa-Lobos (1887-1959) was a famous composer
Gilberto Freyre (1900-), a writer and sociologist
Lúcio Costa (1902-) was the architect who designed Brasília
Cândido Portinari (1903-62) was an artist, famous for his wall paintings
Roberto Burle Marx (1909-94), was a garden designer, artist and botanist
Jorge Amado (1912-), a journalist, politician and novelist
Maria Bueno (1939-), a tennis player
Pelé (1940-), a world famous footballer
Gilberto Gil (1945-), a musician
Francisco Mendez (1944-88) led a campaign to save the rainforests
Ayrton Senna (1960-94) was a world champion racing driver

Some key events in history

1500: the Portuguese Admiral, Cabral, landed in Brazil
1549: Salvador became the main town of colonial government
1554: the Jesuits established a mission at São Paulo
1565: Río de Janeiro was founded
1763: Río de Janeiro became capital
1789: revolt against the Portuguese led by Tiradentes
1807: Prince Regent (the future King João VI) landed in Brazil
1822: independence declared, and Dom Pedro I became emperor
1840: Emperor Dom Pedro II crowned
1850: the slave trade was banned
1864-70: war with Paraguay
1888: all slaves were freed
1889: Dom Pedro II was deposed, and Brazil became a republic
1912: the rubber boom collapsed
1930: a military coup put Getúlio Vargas into power
1945: Vargas forced to resign
1956: Juscelino Kubitschek elected president
1960: the new capital, Brasília, was inaugurated
1964: the start of 21 years of military dictatorship
1970s: Brazil's economic 'miracle'
1984: Itaipú Dam opened
1985: return to civilian rule
1989: the first direct presidential elections. Collor elected president
1994: Fernando Henrique Cardoso became president

Index